The

Happy Family

Book

A series of verses chronicling the lives
of Ken and Maureen Happy and their
children Darren and Tracey

Property of
Miss Binkley

Written by Geoff Sims

Illustrated by Ray Aggett

© Four S Publishing

10 St Mary's Street Bedford MK42 0AS

ISBN No: 0 9525364 0 4

First published in 1995

Typeset and printed by Stamford Calligraphics, Ufford, Lincs

Preface

These verses tell us all about
The Happy Family
The people don't exist - and yet
They're just like you and me

You'll read about their ups and downs
The things they say and do
And as you read, we hope you'll find
The verses ringing true

For life is odd; so often laughs
Yet frequently it's sad
But mostly we believe that it
Is seldom really bad

And our advice to everyone
Whatever mood you're in
No matter what your circumstance
Just do your best to grin

For maximum enjoyment.....

We hope you like these verses
We hope you'll think them fun
For they're designed to make you smile
When all is said and done

The poetry's old fashioned
You'll find that out in time
The metre's right, and we're convinced
Lines two and four all rhyme

For maximum enjoyment
Here's our advice today
Read every po-em out aloud
And in a 'sing-song' way

Enjoy the Happy family
They're fictional it's true
But maybe stories of their lives
Will 'ring a bell' with you

Ken - on first meeting Maureen

Met this super girl on Sunday
Saw her walking on the pier
Stopped and asked her what the time was
Asked what she was doing here

She said she was just out walking
Taking in the clean sea air
She was with her friend Patricia
But she'd not much time to spare

She is blonde and very pretty
And her name is Maureen Frame
I said - mainly to impress her -
"Maureen is my favourite name"

I pretended to be macho
Boldly asked her for a date
She said "yes" provided that I
Wouldn't keep her out too late

So we're meeting up next Friday
At 'The Bell' at half past eight
Don't know what we'll do together
All I know is I can't wait

Maureen - on first meeting Ken

Walking on the pier on Sunday
As the bells began to chime
Met this boy - he must be stupid
Cos' he couldn't tell the time

He asked me what I was doing
Just as if he didn't know
After all, the pier's restricting
Never very far to go

Asked my name, I wouldn't tell him
'Til he tried to make a guess
Said he liked the name of Maureen
Who's he trying to impress?

Told me that his name is Ken, and
Then he asked me for a date
Went all red and stammered badly
Said we shouldn't stay out late

So I said I'd meet him Friday
At 'The Bell' at half past eight
He seems nice and not too spotty
Truth to tell I just can't wait

Mums - on Ken and Maureen

Ken is acting very strangely
And it really makes me laugh
Started using after-shave, and
Yesterday he had a bath

Preens himself before the mirror
Scrubs his teeth 'til pearly white
Guess he's found himself a girlfriend
Hope she'll think that he's alright

Maureen's found herself a fella'
All the tell-tale signs are there
Given up the stew and dumplings
Now she worries what to wear

Goes around as in a daydream
Saying "Don't I look a sight?"
I just hope that he is worth it
Hope he'll be her Mr Right

Ken - on Maureen

I've been going out with Maureen
On and off for quite a while
We both get on well together
Share a joke and share a smile

We like going to the pictures
Or out drinking at a bar
Meeting friends, or ten-pin bowling
Expeditions in the car

Sometimes we go to a disco
Though I'm not a Fred Astaire
People laugh when I start dancing
They make fun but I don't care

Stumble round the crowded dance floor
'Specially when I've had a few
Maureen never stops complaining
Says her feet get black and blue

At the cinema it's lovely
Sitting kissing in the dark
So romantic, so exciting
And it's warmer than the park

Me and Maureen are 'an item'
Must confess that it suits me
We spend all our time together
Tweedledum and Tweedledee

Every day I want her with me
Every moment we should share
She's my dream, my inspiration -
Can I be in love with her?

Maureen - on her engagement

Open up the champagne, Mother
I've got news that just can't wait
Ken and I are getting married
And we've set a wedding date

Yes, he made a true proposal
On one knee, romantic'lly
Then he went and split his trousers
And he blamed it all on me

After we'd got over laughing
I agreed to be his bride
We'll get married next September
Ken and Maureen - side by side

Hope you'll give us your approval
Means a lot to both of us
And tell Dad that it won't cost much
'Cos we don't want too much fuss!

Maureen - on changing her name

I've waited such a long time
To change my name from Frame
For truth to tell, I must confess
I've never liked that name

For frames belong to spectacles
And playgrounds in the park
And pictures hanging on the walls
My friends think it's a lark

But now I've met this lovely boy
And we both fell in love
His name, though it's unusual
Just fits me like a glove

For Happy is his surname and
Perhaps it means love's blind
For our engagement puts me in
A Happy/Frame of mind

I feel elated, full of joy
Ecstatic through and through
Cos' now I'm happy in my heart
And on my passport too!

Ken - on the eve of his wedding

'Tis our wedding day tomorrow
Time of fun and jollity
Yet I am a soul in torment
Asking questions endlessly

Will we like the house we've chosen?
Will we live there happily?
Can we pay the rates and mortgage?
When to start a family?

I'm concerned about my in-laws
Should I call your father 'Dad'?
Will your parents learn to trust me
Like the son they never had

Will I have to dig the garden?
Decorate? Or mend a fuse?
Wash the dishes? Change a light bulb?
Prune the roses? Clean the shoes?

Put up shelves? Or clean the windows?
Lag the pipes? Or mend a pan?
I'm not good at D.I.Y., and
I am not a handyman

Must I learn to love your parrot
He and I are not at ease
All that trilling drives me mad, and
Psittacosis makes me sneeze

What about my football matches?
Up to now they've been my right
Can I keep my independence
With the lads on Friday night?

They're my doubts but do not worry
I'll be at the church for you
We will find out all the answers
We will make our dreams come true

We'll get married in the morning
We will both declare "I do"
Then we'll share our lives together
You and me - and parrot too!

Maureen - on her wedding eve

'Tis our wedding day tomorrow
Time of fun and jollity
Kenneth, you should know just what a
Happy girl you're making me

I'm excited, I'm so happy
Know you feel the same way too
We were made for one another
I can't wait to say I do

But of course I've got some worries
How I wish I was like you
You're so calm and so unruffled
So controlled, it isn't true

I can't help but think of questions
It's my nature I suppose
Will it rain tomorrow morning?
Will you like the dress I chose?

Will the wedding car be shiny?
I just hope I won't be late
Will the bridesmaids walk in step, and
Will my head dress stay on straight

Will we like the wedding pictures?
Will the best man's speech be rude?
Will the caterer be ready?
Will your mother like the food?

You will be a loving husband
Honouring our wedding vows
Will you spend your leisure moments
Doing jobs around the house?

When I see you with my parrot -
Loving him the way you do -
I just know that we'll be happy
Cos' that's how you love me too!

Just think, from tomorrow morning
You and I are man and wife
Lovers, sweethearts, always sharing
Happiness in married life

Ken - on the birth of Darren

"A son" they said, "you've got a son"
My heart fair burst with joy
For girls are special, but you know
There's no-one like a boy

A boy plays football, fishes, skates
Digs holes and climbs up trees
Gets stung, gets dirty, cuts his lip
Tears clothes and scrapes his knees

He'll try to bully, start a fight
And get a bloody nose
He'll challenge my authority
And keep me on my toes

There'll be no peace while he's around
My patience will get shorter
Perhaps my life would easier be
If we had had a daughter!

Darren - on his own Christening

They took me to Church in the morning
Asleep - with a smile on my face
As it was my Christening Service
They'd dressed me in satin and lace
I woke up and yawned, looked around me
"Oh what a sweet infant" they said
Then a man in what looked like a night shirt
Splashed water all over my head
I didn't react to that kindly
Cos' I'm not a meek little chap
I cried and I screamed in a tantrum
And Mum had to give me a slap

The vicar became quite indignant
"This child is just naughty I think"
So I burped and was sick down his surplice
And made the most horrible stink
A man from a neighbouring family
Who thought my behaviour a lark
Collapsed in a fit of amusement
And made an un-Christian remark
The Christening service was over
It closed with the usual hymn
But I know that I'll always remember
The font where I first learned to swim!

Ken - on helping to bath Darren

I helped to bath baby today
We all had a wonderful time
The bathroom rang loudly with laughter
It was just like our own pantomime

It gave me a warm tender feeling
To cradle our child in my arm
He looked up with eyes that were trusting
He knew that he'd come to no harm

We splashed and we laughed and we giggled
We made the bath water quite rough
He didn't want me to stop playing
But Mummy said that was enough

It was a most happy occasion
With water all over the place
And the chuckles of our little baby
Were as warm as the smile on his face

It gave me the sweetest of mem'ries
And one that I'll never forget
That day that I helped to bath baby
- And I was the one who got wet!

Ken - on buying a car

Car's been making funny noises
So we wonder what to do
Shall we swap to something bigger?
Shall we part exchange for new?

Shall we stay with make and model
We have had for many a year
Or try one entirely diff'rent
One that has an extra gear

What about the size of engine
Carburettor? BHP?
Please explain about unleaded
- All this technicality

Cornering and size of wheelbase
Tell me more about the ride
What's that Maureen? Yes I've noticed
It looks bright and smart inside

Maureen's more concerned with colour
She can choose from every hue
And she thinks a sunshine roof is
Also most important too

Carpet pile and stereo system
But one factor will decide
What's the size and shape of boot, and
Will her shopping fit inside

Our concerns are not the same, but
We'll agree eventually
And I bet that, come the signing
That will all be left to me!

Maureen - on Darren's first tooth

Baby's cut a tooth today
Clever little lad
Soon he'll start on solids
Meat and veg' like Dad

No wonder he's been fractious
Miserable and glum
It must be very painful
When tooth first comes through gum!

Better make provision
See Insurance man
Think about the future
Start a dental plan!

Maureen - on the birth of Tracey

Darren come into my bedroom
There's someone I want you to see
You've got a brand new baby sister
I hope that you'll love her, like me

Just look at her; isn't she pretty?
Her sweet little mouth and her nose
The way that she crinkles her face up
Her ten tiny fingers and toes

Darren, she's not 'red and wrinkled'
I won't have you calling her that
And I prefer calling her 'cuddly'
To saying she's 'ugly and fat!'

Darling don't show her your tadpoles
She's little, she won't understand
And no, you can't offer her biscuits
Just look at the state of your hand

We're planning on calling her Tracey
I think that's a nice name, don't you?
What's that you're saying? No, really
I don't think she'd suit 'Looby Loo'

When she's older she'll be very pretty
And I bet you'll be very proud
Though she'll be surrounded by others
She'll always stand out in the crowd

Until then take care of your sister
And see that she comes to no grief
I'll make sure you get all her fruitcake
- At least 'til she gets all her teeth!

Darren - on going to school

My Mummy says I cried and cried
On my first day at school
And looking back I s'pose I was
A silly little fool

For school was good and school was fun
With other girls and boys
We played with plasticine and paint
And lots of lovely toys

We painted pictures, sang some songs
Said lots of nursery rhymes
We ate our dinners, learned to read -
They were such happy times

When I look back I s'pose that I
Just cried 'cos I was sad
I'd never been to school before
And I missed Mum and Dad

Darren - on breaking a window

Can I have a word with you Mummy?
I hope that you've had a good day
For something quite awful has happened
And you need to know right away

They do say that 'accidents happen'
And I know that that's very true
'Cos this morning an accident happened
And it's one that affects me and you

I picked up this stone in the garden
It was lying right there in the sand
When all of a sudden the wind blew
And the stone flew right out of my hand

Now none of this ought to have happened
But please let me have my short say
'Cos as that stone flew like a bullet
A window got right in the way!

So when you go into the kitchen
A window all broken you'll see
I'm sorry to say I'm the culprit
The window was broken by me

Ken - on Darren's first bike

We gave you your first bike this morning
And watched your eyes light up with joy
For owning a brand new two wheeler
Is the dream of a six year old boy

We looked at the wheels and the chassis
The handlebar, pedals and bell
The chain and the brakes and reflector
We pumped up the tyres as well

You then rode with me close beside you
My hand firm and strong at your side
At last came your turn to ride solo
And Mum and I watched you with pride

Take care of your bike and be careful
It'll serve you for many a mile
Ride straight and watch out for life's pot-holes
Face up to each puncture and smile

Be good to your friends and your family
And perhaps in another five years
We'll buy you a bike for a grown-up
A racer with seventeen gears

Maureen - on Darren's euphonium

Today I'm far from happy
In fact I'm feeling glum
My son has come home from his school
With a euphonium

He's not a very big boy
He's small, and rather slim
And frankly his euphonium
Is twice as big as him

He said he's got to practice
He makes a frightful din
The neighbours are complaining
And calling it a sin

The noise is loud and painful
It hurts my aching head
He'll have to go and practice in
A sound proofed garden shed!

Ken - on a day in the park

Quite often the whole Happy fam'ly
Goes out for a walk by the lake
But last time we went was disastrous
I'm sorry for everyone's sake

The children were full of excitement
To feed all the ducks and the swans
We took half a loaf and some pastry
And six of my wife's home-made scones

The bread was all eaten with relish
But when I threw in the first scone
The ducks all flew off broken-hearted
Except for one foolhardy swan

The swan was both brave and courageous
A beak-full of scone he did take
He swallowed it, then he flipped over
And sank to the bed of the lake

A tramp, passing by, got excited
"I'm hungry, please feed me" he cried
He bit on a scone and turned purple
He choked - and I thought he had died

We walked to the bridge o'er the river
And threw in the scones with bad grace
A smart little motorised cruiser
Was hit - and just sank without trace

The moral of this little story
Is that, to avoid tragedy
We must bar my wife from the kitchen
And eat only biscuits for tea!

Darren - on a day off school

I was sick at school today
Brought up all my dinner
Yet somehow I'm sure that I
Don't seem any thinner

Mum says I must go to bed
Rest my poor digestion
So, when can I eat again?
Is the burning question

I lie in bed with hunger pains
Gnawing at my tummy
I can't wait 'til morning. "Can I
Have some biscuits, Mummy?"

Darren - on being given a kitten

Dad came home from work today
With a little cat
Not much more than three months old
Fluffy, round and fat
Said it was a gift for me
I'd been good to Mother
Thought the cat would help me learn
Kindness to each other
Pets remind us all the time
That we need to care
Feed them, give them lots to drink
Give them love to share

So I'm taking care of cat
With his fur like silk
Give him tinned food every day
Saucers full of milk
Sneak him extra special snacks
Keep his tummy full
Play with him for hours and hours
With a ball of wool
Love my cat - his name is Tom
- Never call him Mog
But I often wish that Dad
Had brought me home a dog

Tracey - on her best friend

My best friend is Rachel Thomas
She lives seven doors from me
We do everything together
She is five and I am three

People say we look like sisters
Though I'm not a bit like her
She wears skirts and woolly jumpers
I am dark and she is fair

Every day we play together
Give our dollies cups of tea
Sometimes Rachel tells me stories
She can read a bit, you see

We go to the shops with Mummy
Walk together hand in hand
Rachel knows what all the things are
I don't always understand

Rachel's started learning ballet
Hopes to end up on the stage
Mummy says that I can join, too
When I get to Rachel's age

Sometimes Rachel makes me jealous
All she has to say is "please"
Mummy tells me, when I ask, that
Money doesn't grow on trees

I love Rachel very dearly
And I'll always feel that way
We'll be happy ever after
And that's how we'll always stay

Ken - on noises in the night

Woke one night with heart a-pounding
What's that noise that I can hear?
Half past two and wind is howling
I am paralysed with fear

Lie there hoping I've been dreaming
It's my over-active brain
Maybe just imagination
No - I hear it once again

Maureen whispers "Don't just lie there
Go down and investigate
After all we could be burgled
While you just prevaricate!"

Creep downstairs with torch a-shining
Hear the noise again, "What's that?"
Are they dangerous intruders?
No - it's only Darren's cat!

Tracey - on Christmas Eve

I've got my eyes so tightly shut
And I've tried counting sheep
But still I lie here wide awake
I just can't get to sleep

It's so important that I soon
Am fast asleep in bed
Or Father Christmas may not come
A-calling on his sled

For its a rule he always keeps
Of this make no mistake
He never calls on boys and girls
If they are still awake

I hope he'll bring me books and toys
A nurse's uniform
A pram, some skates, a Cindy doll
And gloves to keep me warm

But first I must get off to sleep
The trying drives me mad
Hush! Who's that coming? Is it Santa?
No - it's only Dad

Maureen - on Christmas

Christmas is a time of kindness
Giving presents, having fun
Stretching out the hand of friendship
Peace on earth to everyone

In our house it isn't like that
Not my favourite time of year
Tempers fray and tension mounts as
Festive season's drawing near

It's a nice, long held tradition
We all dress the Christmas tree
Fairy lights come out of storage
Never work first time for me

Presents stored in secret places
How we 'practise to deceive'
I do Christmas shopping early
Kenneth waits 'til Christmas Eve

Plan the menu for an army
Freezer's full to overflow
Wines and spirits by the litre
Where does all the money go?

Church bells ringing Christmas morning
Presents opened by the score
Bags of crumpled wrapping paper
Messing up my tidy floor

Dinner time around the table
Christmas crackers, festive scene
Turkey, stuffing, Christmas pudding
Hurry - or we'll miss the Queen

Sausages and cold roast turkey
Doesn't anyone want more?
Liver salts and alka seltzer
Friends come knocking at the door

All that work and all that bother
And it makes me wonder, why?
'Specially when I know that I've been
Planning for it since July

Tracey - on being given a pony

Dad's promised to buy me a pony
It's true; yes he told me today
The promise was so unexpected
I just didn't know what to say

I'm thrilled and I'm very excited
I love him; he's so good to me
I should have thanked Dad for his kindness
But words don't come that easily

I wonder where we'll keep the pony
- A field where she'll frolic and play
And we'll have to think about feeding
She'll need lots of oats and some hay

I'll need lots of riding equipment
And boots that come up to my knees
A saddle and all kinds of harness
And Mum says "They don't grow on trees!"

I'll have to decide what to call her
Like 'Muffin', or 'Champion' or 'Bess'
Perhaps she'll resemble a 'Snowball'
'Black Beauty' or maybe 'Black Bess'

I could call her something like 'Lucky'
But that's not the right name you see
It won't be the pony who's lucky
Oh no, 'cos the lucky one's me!

Maureen - on a family picnic

Pack the picnic basket
Lots of things to eat
Pies and pickled gherkins
Savoury and sweet

Salads and cucumbers
Pate, eggs and ham
Crisps and pickled onions
Pots of home made jam

Cakes and flans and pastries
Scores of sausage rolls
Apples and bananas
Cups and plates and bowls

Cans of beer and lager
Wine - both white and red
Lemonade and soda
Lightly buttered bread

Mustard, salt and pepper
Hardly worth a glance
Indigestion tablets
Nothing left to chance

Pack the car with goodies
Rugs and plastic sheet
And a faded sunshade
To withstand the heat

Going to the seaside
To enjoy the sun
Happy family picnic
Lots and lots of fun

Stop! What's this I see now
On the window pane?
Flaming English weather
Spots of falling rain

Tracey - on a trip to the circus

Daddy took us to the circus
Mummy came, and Darren too
Animals, performing tricks, were
Cleverer than in the Zoo

Dogs and bears and wily monkeys
Animals of every size
Shiny seals with 'clapping' flippers
Did their tricks before my eyes

Acrobats of all descriptions
Dressed in costumes, masks and veils
Line of elephants came trudging
Holding one anothers' tails

Ladies in their spangled sequins
Riding horses, stood bareback
Laughing clowns in baggy trousers
Gave each other such a whack

Then the terrifying tigers
Gave me such a fearful fright
Showed their teeth and roared at keepers
I stayed hidden - out of sight

Finally a thrilling climax
Trumpets sound and drummers roll
As a man walked on a tight rope
Holding just a shiny pole

Circus life would suit me nicely
Teaching creatures to behave
But I couldn't handle tigers
I could never be that brave

Ken - on a trip to the seaside

We went to the seaside last Tuesday
My Maureen, the children and me
It wasn't a happy experience
We left at a quarter to three

I paid £2.50 to park in
A field half a mile from the beach
And Darren dropped one of his trainers
In a rock pool, just out of my reach

The weather was sunless and raining
The cold gave my Maureen chapped lips
For lunch we made do with a plateful
Of soggy fish fingers and chips

I bought all the family an ice cream
But mine slipped right out of my hand
And slithered all down my best trousers
To land upside down in the sand

We all spent an hour at the funfair
With hot dogs and sherbet to lick
The rides were all far too expensive
And Tracey and Darren were sick

The tide was far out in the distance
Exposing an acre of mud
The kids said they wanted to paddle
And, stupidly, I said they could

In no time at all they were stranded
And Maureen soon started to fret
So I had to go to their rescue
And got my best trousers all wet

We packed up and came home quite early
And truth to tell little was said
For I made it clear from my silence
I'd rather have stayed home in bed

Darren - on things he dislikes

I hate waking very early
When it's cold and dark and wet
I hate baths and toads and cornflakes
And when Mother calls me 'pet'

I hate school and little sisters
I hate piano lessons too
I hate shops and paper rounds and
Family outings to the zoo

I hate washing up the dishes
I hate polishing my shoes
I hate Wimbledon and cricket
And when Man United lose

I hate sprouts and mashed potatoes
Fatty meat that's found in stew
I hate Church and Sunday School and
All the things that children do

I can't wait to be a grown up
That's the best time I've been told
In the meantime all I know is
I hate being twelve years old

Ken - on the need for a hobby

Here's a thought that I feel is important
I hope that you'll show your accord
I believe that young folk should have hobbies
For that way they'll never get bored

For a hobby helps keep our minds active
At least that's what I always find
It helps to keep idle hands busy
Idle hand often makes idle mind

And as to your choice of a hobby
Well that is as wide as can be
Consider and make your selection
I'm sure that you'll quickly agree

A hobby enthrals and enriches
I don't think my feelings are wrong
Choose wisely and you'll find a hobby
Will stay with you all your life long

Ken - on being the victim of flu'

I went to the Doctor last Tuesday
Although I'm quite healthy you know
The wife said she needs a prescription
And foolishly I said I'd go

I sat in the waiting room, waiting
(It's what the room's for, I suppose)
And all around people were sneezing
And coughing, and blowing their nose

I could feel all the germs flying round me
In my mouth, up my nose, in the air
They were marching all over the carpet
And climbing the legs of my chair

I got the prescription, but sadly
I picked up the flu' germ as well
So as a result I feel rotten
Confined to my bed for a spell

As I lie here, with temperature rising
I declare it's a very rum do
That a fit man can go to the Doctor
And end up in bed with the flu'

Darren - on homework

We all complain 'bout homework
But as a gen'ral rule
The homework we should do at home
Is really done at school

It all sounds rather crazy
And Dad can't understand
But we've got lots of periods
With free time on our hands

What makes it even better
Is, if the homework's hard,
We ask our mates for answers
Some one will 'mark our card'

Now some may call that cheating
But I say that's not on
It's pooling our resources
Two heads improve on one

Darren - on a football match

Going to the match tomorrow
Get the scarf and rattle out
Better give my throat a gargle
Be prepared to sing and shout

It's well known that we're the champions
Sing about it every week
Though the team's now in the doldrums
Very soon they'll hit their peak

We've just bought a brand new striker
He'll be wearing number nine
Cost the club a tidy fortune
Took him seven days to sign

We'll support our team forever
They will never walk alone
Win or lose we'll never falter
We can cheer - or we can moan

Tracey - on Easter eggs

Chocolate covered Easter eggs
Are very good to eat
And I consider them to be
A very special treat

But first comes an exciting game
That sometimes takes all day
We have to find the eggs that have
Been hidden well away

They're up the chimney, in the wardrobe
Underneath a bed
In a cupboard, under stairs
Or in the garden shed

I love this game and I don't care
If eggs are hard to find
It adds to the excitement so
I never ever mind

But this year things were not the same
As round the house we run
An Aunt of ours joined in the game
And went and spoiled the fun

For, trying to be kind, she went
And gave us easy clues
So we could quickly find the eggs
And none of us would lose

Within an hour we'd found the lot
And all that I can say
Is - when it's Easter time next year -
I hope she'll stay away

Maureen - on Easter

Easter is a time of pleasure
Christian festival in Spring
Jesus sacrificed for sinners
Hymns and anthems church choirs sing

In the garden buds are bursting
Dormant plants show signs of life
All Gods creatures get together
Every 'husband' takes a 'wife'

Easter means a time of weddings
And the start of warmer days
Easter eggs and Easter bunnies
Games that every family plays

Yes I get a glow of pleasure
As at Easter time I pray
That we'll rise to new beginnings
From the depths of yesterday

Tracey - on finding a holiday job

My holiday employment's in
A leading High Street store
The customers are friendly but
The work can be a bore

I tidy up the storeroom and
I count and check the stock
I answer questions all the time
From nine to five o'clock

I'm glad that I am working, but
It's not a job I'd seek
And pay-day is the one day I
Look forward to each week

Darren - on his hairy chest

I was drying myself after having a bath
When I looked down and saw with surprise
There's a single hair growing right there on my chest
I could hardly believe my two eyes

Now I know that it's usual for men to grow hair
And often it grows thick and strong
But the first one to grow is the best of them all
Will it be dark and curly and long?

I've a long way to go to Neanderthal Man
And I still feel quite naked and bare
But I feel kind of proud as I stand and I stroke
That one, special, solitary hair

Darren - on job hunting

Dad says I must face the future
Soon I will be leaving school
I must look for work or I'll be
In the unemployment pool

I'm not sure for what I'm suited
Where does my ambition stop?
Should I concentrate on training?
Will I make it to the top

Should I join an old profession?
Doctor, lawyer, architect?
What to do, and how to do it?
Where my talents to direct?

Should I write to firms, or go through
An Employment Agency?
Should I look at ads in papers?
Which way is the best for me?

Tinker, Tailor, Soldier, Sailor
Which job will I do the best?
I could try my hand at driving
Once I've passed my driving test!

Truth to tell I'm not that fussy
Nor am I an empty shell
I just want a job that's easy
One that pays me very well

Ken - on sitting in the sun

Gard'ning finished; jobs all done
Hurry out into the sun
Loungers waiting, mattress laid
A parasol to give some shade

Books a'plenty, drinks with ice
Very peaceful, very nice
Lying there we start to yawn
'Til thoughtless neighbour mows his lawn

Sleep disturbed but lie in sun
'Til scores of insects spoil our fun
Wasps and hornets, dragon flies
Horse flies, bees of every size

Noisy children all around
Making an unpleasant sound
I know they just want to play
But why can't they all play away?

How we grumble and complain -
Then behold it starts to rain
Wonder why we lose our tether
In this English summer weather

Darren - on his first flight

My head is a-pounding
My mouth has gone dry
I feel that I just want
To break down and cry

And what is the reason
For my sorry plight
Today is the day I
Must make my first flight

I've packed up my suitcase
And been to the 'loo'
The taxi is ordered
For quarter to two

Then off to the airport
And straight to the bar
For drinking makes flying
Much easier by far

I spend the flight sitting
All tense in my seat
I doubt if I'll ever
Stand up on my feet

At last we have landed
And come to no grief
I loosen my seat belt
And laugh with relief

I tell myself that I've
Been silly to fret
And work myself up to
A lathering sweat

For flying is easy
There's no need to fuss
But if Spain was nearer
I'd go there by bus

Tracey - on Spring

Spring's my very favourite season
Shrubs and trees burst into bud
Yellow daffodils and tulips
- Suddenly the world looks good

In the fields the new lambs gambol
Hedgerows turn a shade of green
Birds and bees all go a-courting
Mother Nature now is Queen

Spring time heralds in a new year
Time when life begins anew
Summer now is round the corner
Grey skies looking much more blue

Winter ends, new life beginning
Birds build nests and learn to sing
Nodding bluebell heads are ringing
Gentle, good, life-giving Spring

Ken - on sleepless nights

I lie in bed for hours at night
And try to put the world to right
And try to rectify each sad mistake

But all the while it seems to me
Solutions don't come easily
And they just end up keeping me awake

Then, as the hours advance through night
Sleep comes at last and makes things right
I slumber on until the light of day

And when I waken in the morn
Refreshed - just like a child, new born
I find my problems have all gone away

Maureen - on Tracey's driving test

Daddy and I were so sorry
To learn of the setback you've had
The Driving Examiner's failed you
And darling, it's really too bad

However just look on the bright side
For matters could be a lot worse
Cos' you might have hit a steamroller
Instead of that six year old hearse!

The Police are unlikely to charge you
And there is more good news to share
The Driving Examiner's better -
He's moved out of intensive care

The Bodyshop man says the Astra
Will soon be as sound as a bell
The stain on the seat can't be shifted
At least we've got rid of the smell

So cheer up, be happy and thankful
And pour out a glass of champagne
Cos' after a dozen more lessons
You could take the test once again!

Tracey - on exam results

At last exams are over
That was the easy part
Now many weeks of waiting
Will test my patient heart
Anxiety is rampant
And questions cause a mood
While nervous indigestion
Just puts me off my food
The fam'ly says "don't worry"
I know that they mean well
But there's a lot at stake here
And only time will tell

I've said it doesn't matter
I've tried to play it cool
But I don't relish failure
Don't want to look a fool
These beastly weeks of waiting
May send me off the rails
But I'll continue pacing
And chewing on my nails
At last results are published
Announce them cheerfully
Better than I'd hoped for
Two A's and a B!

Darren - on dental treatment

It's seven fifteen in the morning
And soon I must rise from my sleep
Get dressed and get washed, have my breakfast
For I've an appointment to keep

Today I must go to the dentist
For he has five fillings to do
And he has decided that treatment
Is now many months overdue

He'll give me a painful injection
Then after my senses are numb
He'll fill up my mouth with his gadgets
And ask "What's the weather like, chum?"

He'll drill 'til I'm sure that he's digging
A deep almost bottomless hole
Then calmly suggest that I might like
To spit in his stainless steel bowl

It's at times like this that prevention
Seems very much better than cure
So perhaps a six-monthly inspection
Is something I ought to endure

Tracey - on a special holiday

The sun and the sand and the seagulls
The restaurant where we first met
The bar where you bought me a brandy
They're mem'ries I'll never forget

We danced every night 'neath the moonlight
We boogied right through 'til the dawn
One morning I woke with a headache
To find that I'd slept on the lawn

The hotel we shared was delightful
With pool and sun loungers galore
We spent every day in the sunshine
'Til bodies were peeling and sore

We kissed and caressed and canoodled
We danced very close, cheek to cheek
And thinking of all that you told me
Just makes my knees go really weak

It was a most magical fortnight
And I'd like some more of the same
I'd ask you to come with me next year
But I can't remember your name!

Ken - on hearing his alarm clock

Each morning at six thirty
When I'm asleep in bed
My Taiwanese alarm clock
Goes off right by my head

It makes a fearful racket
Enough to wake the dead
There's no way I'd sleep through it
So I get up instead

It always seems the loudest
When I've not had much sleep
Then suddenly it's ringing
And out of bed I leap

I know I'm very lazy
I know I sleep too well
But that Taiwan alarm clock
Is my idea of hell

But when I'm on my holiday
And I don't have a care
With no alarm, I still wake up
It really isn't fair!

Tracey - on finding a true love

Forget the old loves past and gone
The troubles and the strife
For now I've found the man with whom
I want to share my life

We've bought the ring and pledged our love
For ever and a day
The love we share is strong, and it
Will always stay that way

He's kind and thoughtful, gentle too
Good natured, full of care
We've lots of common interests
So many things we share

He's handsome, fun to be with, and
He never makes me sad
I think I like him best cos' he
Reminds me of my Dad

Ken - on giving Tracey away

I write these verses just to say
I was so proud of you today
As I walked with you down the aisle
And you gave me your special smile
Your beauty, elegance and grace
So self assured and fair of face
The way you walked, so straight and tall
- No wonder you impressed us all
The way you stood at altar rail
The little girl I once thought frail
Now grown up, strong and forthright too
Prepared to say the words "I do"

The way you took your husband's hand
As if in fairy wonderland
The look you gave him, warm and real
That told him of the way you feel
The way you greeted everyone
With friendly smile and word of fun
The poise you showed throughout the day
'Till all the guests had gone away
And now you've got another's name
But I will love you just the same
I'll think about you come what may
-The daughter that I gave away!

Maureen - on Tracey's wedding

I'm sometimes sad at weddings
I sometimes shed a tear
And this one's no exception
For Tracey's very dear

It's not that I'm unhappy
Or worried in my heart
It's more a sense of happiness
That makes the crying start

Today, though, I'm determined
That I will cry no more
I'll welcome to the family
A loving son-in-law

I'm such a lucky mother
Cos' when all's said and done
I haven't lost a daughter
I've found an extra son

Darren - on being in love

When will I feel such elation?
When will I drink richer wine?
When will I savour the taste and the flavour
Of grapes newly picked from the vine

When will the moon shine so brightly?
When will the nightingale sing?
When will I see delicate symmetry
Like the pattern on butterfly's wing?

When will the fragrance of freezias?
Touch on my sensitive nose?
Like Chanel Number Five, honey fresh from the hive
Or the smell of a sweet scented rose?

When will I hear nicer music?
When will I feel such romance?
When will I capture the joy and the rapture
Of you in my arms as we dance?

These are my most tender mem'ries
I long to recall them, but when?
The answer it's true lies only with you
T'will be when you kiss me again!

Ken - after Tracey's marriage

We're thinking of having a lodger
'Cos daughter got married today
And now we've a spare second bedroom
We might as well make the room pay

The rent that we get will be useful
T'will bring us some comfort and cheer
A bottle of gin and some choc'lates
A crate of best Heineken beer

We'll make the digs sound most attractive
BB and a good evenin' meal
Home comforts and every convenience
At twelve quid a week - quite a deal

We're not sure just who we should look for
"Professional man'" says the wife
But I rather fancy a female
To brighten my dull boring life

So let's make a toast, raise our glasses
And let's give three cheers, hip hooray
To enterprise, freedom - but mostly
To the daughter who married today

Ken - on holidays with Maureen

Do you remember long before
The children called the tune?
We used to holiday alone
Beneath a lovers' moon
We'd spend all day and half the night
Together, hand in hand
We'd seek a nice secluded beach
With palms and golden sand
I'd tell you that I loved you and
We'd kiss, our hearts entwined
Would beat as one, together then
In body and in mind

But then the kids came on the scene
Our holidays were changed
We had to firstly think of them
Our lives were re-arranged
For many years it's been that way
But now they've grown, perchance
We'll get back to those good old days
And resurrect romance
We'll rediscover all those things
We knew and liked before
And I just know that we will find
We love each other more

Ken - on getting older

I've not been feeling well
I've got this painful knee
And Doctor says he thinks I should
Have physiotherapy

I tried a course of treatment which
Worked well up to a point
As skilled massage and exercise
Relieved my aching joint

But time is no great healer as
Along the way it races
I soon found out that I'd got pains
In lots of other places

I've always been a healthy chap
No asthma or bronchitis
But now the Doctor thinks that I've
Got osteo-arthritis!

Tracey - on her parents

I'm married now and I must learn
To lead a different life
To love and care for someone else
To be a perfect wife

But always I'll be grateful for
The start in life I had
My close, supportive family
The love of Mum and Dad

You'll be my inspiration, in
My mem'ry constantly
A wonderful example of
What married life should be

And though I've changed my name, and we
May live so far apart
I know that I will always be
A Happy girl at heart

Ken - on being made redundant

I was called into the office
Sad at heart and feeling low
Boss said "Sorry, orders falling
I will have to let you go!"

"Let me go?" I asked in wonder
He explained just what he meant
Didn't like to say 'redundant'
It's a rotten sentiment

I won't get a golden handshake
I'm expected to 'make do'
I just have to join the millions
In the unemployment queue

Jobs are scarce and there's a prospect
I may never work again
But there's nothing gained from mis'ry
And I never will complain

For as Maureen says, I'm healthy
And I've love from one who cares
And if work is what I'm after
I can paint the hall and stairs

Maureen - on the weather

There is something to be said
For a soft, warm, feather bed
On a cold and frosty, wild and wintry night

And it's great if you perspire
By a roaring log-wood fire
As the snow falls down and everywhere is white

And a glass or two that cheers
Is sweet music to my ears
While the fog's obscuring everything in sight

But I'm happier to recall
That I like it best of all
When our summer sunshine puts the world to right

Darren - on his parents

Dear Mum and Dad, I write to say
That I feel very proud today
To have two parents like you two
Who've helped me make my dreams come true

You've made me laugh, removed my frown
And picked me up when I felt 'down'
You've made me work and helped me play
Supported me in every way

You've taught me what to value most
You've never let me brag or boast
You've taught me to be kind and care
To clean my shoes and brush my hair

Yes, Mum and Dad, it's very true
That everything I owe to you
And your reward? Well, luckily
You've got a son as nice as me!

Ken - on a desert experience

Whilst touring on a holiday
On a Saharan bus
A gang of Arab tribesmen came
Along and menaced us
Their leader was a fearsome man
Dressed in his Arab clothes
He had a weatherbeaten face
Slit eyes and sharp, hooked nose

He eyed my Maureen up and down
And muttered to his men
Then he bent down and picked her up
With Maureen shouting "Ken!"
He swung her up before him on
His lumpy camel's back
Then cracked his whip and they were off
Along the desert track

I wasn't going to stand for that
So, letting out a wail
As he went past I grabbed hold of
His smelly camel's tail
That camel seemed to run for miles
Just dragging me along
The Arab lashed me with his whip
But my grip was too strong

At last they stopped and clustered round
As I lay bleeding there
With sand in every orifice
A picture of despair
The leader leaned down over me
And pulling out a knife
He said he'd give me sixteen goats
If I'd give him my wife

"I'll not agree to that" I cried
At which the Arab cursed
And raising up his vicious knife
Prepared to do his worst
And as the knife descended, I
Awakened from my dream
But not before I'd let out an
Involuntary scream

My wife woke too and soothed me as
I told her of my plight
She was quite touched to learn that I'd
Put up a fearsome fight
"Don't thank me, for to offer sixteen
Goats is rather naughty
Cos' Maureen, dear, a wife like you is
Worth no less than forty!"

Ken - on unfulfilled ambitions

When I was a child my ambition
Was clear cut and easy to see
I wanted to drive a steam roller
Have ice cream and jelly for tea

But then in my teens I just wanted
To travel like Scott to the Pole
To be a top racing car driver
Or play for United in goal

By the time I had got to my twenties
My ambition was much more mature
I wanted to play in a pop group
Or lie on some sunny sea shore

By thirty I'd grown staid and boring
My ambition was now for success
I wanted to be an Accountant
And have an expensive address

Things didn't change when at forty
I thought about my future life
Except that I now thought I'd settle
For a Jag' - and a very rich wife!

At fifty I found my ambitions
Were that of a more mature chap
I wanted to get to retirement
And lower my golf handicap

But now that I've reached age of sixty
Ambition comes more modestly
I just want to be hale and hearty
And live to a hundred and three!

We've now reached the last of these verses
Our saga has come to an end
Maybe - if it's been entertaining -
You'll mention that fact to a friend

Remember the name 'Happy Fam'ly'
Cos' there'll be more stories to tell
For life's full of happy adventures
As we all know only too well